EXTREME SUR[VIVAL]

SURVIVING THE WILDERNESS

Michael Hurley

Raintree

Chicago, Illinois

www.heinemannraintree.com
Visit our website to find out more information about Heinemann-Raintree books.

To order:
☎ Phone 888-454-2279
💻 Visit www.heinemannraintree.com to browse our catalog and order online.

© 2011 Raintree
an imprint of Capstone Global Library, LLC
Chicago, Illinois

Visit our website at
www.heinemannraintree.com

Edited by Adam Miller, Adrian Vigliano, and Andrew Farrow
Designed by Steve Mead
Original illustrations © Capstone Global Library Ltd.
Illustrated by Jeff Edwards and KJA-Artists.com
Picture research by Tracy Cummins
Production by Camilla Crask
Originated by Capstone Global Library Ltd
Printed and bound in the United States of America, North Mankato, MN

15 14 13 12 11
10 9 8 7 6 5 4 3 2 1

Library of Congress Cataloging-in-Publication Data
Hurley, Michael.
   Surviving the wilderness / Michael Hurley.
      p. cm.—(Extreme survival)
   Includes bibliographical references and index.
   ISBN 978-1-4109-3972-2 (hc)
   ISBN 978-1-4109-3979-1 (pb)
   1. Wilderness survival. I. Title.
   GV200.5.H87 2011
   613.6′9—dc22   2010028839

Acknowledgments
The author and publishers are grateful to the following for permission to reproduce copyright material: Alamy pp. **5** (©Aurora Photos), **8** & **9** (©Christian Kapteyn); AP Photo pp. **35**, **4** (E Pablo Kosmicki), **36** top (Guy Magowan/West Australian), **36** bottom (Kerry Berrington); Corbis pp. **42** & **43** (©Frans Lanting), **15** (©Jason Burke/Eye Ubiquitous), **18** & **19** (©Paul Souders), **30** & **31** (©RAFAEL MARCHANTE/Reuters); defenseimagery. mil pp. **16** & **17** (MSGT Rose Reynolds); Evrett Collection, inc. p. **48**; Getty Images pp. **45** (Andy Rouse), **10** & **28** (David Trood), **23** (Jeff Foott), **11** (Susanna Price); Hungry Eye Images p. **25** (Ed Wardle); National Geographic Stock pp. **18** left & **20** (Alaska Stock Images); **29** News Ltd pp. **29** & **44** (©Newspix); Photolibrary pp. **46** & **47** (Chris Cheadle), **33** (Martin Harvey); Shutterstock pp. **14** (©Alexander Yu. Zotov), **27** (©Ralph Loesche), **22** (©Steve Bower), **6** & **7** (©Timothy Epp); ©Steve Callahan pp. **38**, **41**; THE KOBAL COLLECTION p. **13** (FILM FOUR/PATHE/SUTTON-HIBBERT, JEREMY).

Cover photograph of the summit of Mont Blanc reproduced with the permission of Getty Images/ Mario Colonel.

We would like to thank Ann Fullick for her invaluable help in the preparation of this book.

Every effort has been made to contact copyright holders of any material reproduced in this book. Any omissions will be rectified in subsequent printings if notice is given to the publisher.

Disclaimer
All the Internet addresses (URLs) given in this book were valid at the time of going to press. However, due to the dynamic nature of the Internet, some addresses may have changed, or sites may have changed or ceased to exist since publication. While the author and publisher regret any inconvenience this may cause readers, no responsibility for any such changes can be accepted by either the author or the publisher.

CONTENTS

Some words are printed in bold, **like this**. You can find out what they mean by looking in the glossary.

INTO THE WILDERNESS

Aron Ralston managed to survive in the wilderness by cutting off his own hand.

Throughout history, people have always had the desire to explore and discover new places. This has often meant spending time in the wilderness. In this book, you will read stories about people who have overcome incredible challenges and danger while trying to survive in the wilderness.

Going to extremes

One of the most famous stories of surviving in the wilderness is the story of U.S. mountain climber Aron Ralston. While mountain climbing in Utah's Bluejohn Canyon in 2003, a heavy boulder fell on Aron, trapping him by pinning his right arm down. Unable to move, he waited to be rescued, but because no one knew where he was, nobody arrived to help him.

Unbearable pain

After being trapped for six days, Aron decided that the only way he was going to survive was to **amputate** (cut off) his hand that was trapped under the boulder. He snapped the arm at the wrist to break it, and then he used his penknife to cut through the skin, muscle, and nerves. It must have been almost unbearable pain. Aron said afterward: "When I amputated, I felt every bit of it. It hurt to break the bone, and it certainly hurt to cut the nerve. But cutting the muscle was not as bad."

Aron showed a lot of courage and determination. He clearly thought hard about what he could do to help himself survive. Although it was a very extreme decision to cut off his own hand, it almost definitely saved his life.

This is the boulder that trapped Aron, and the spot where he was forced to cut his hand off. You can see blood stains on the stone wall to the right of the boulder.

TRAINING TO SURVIVE

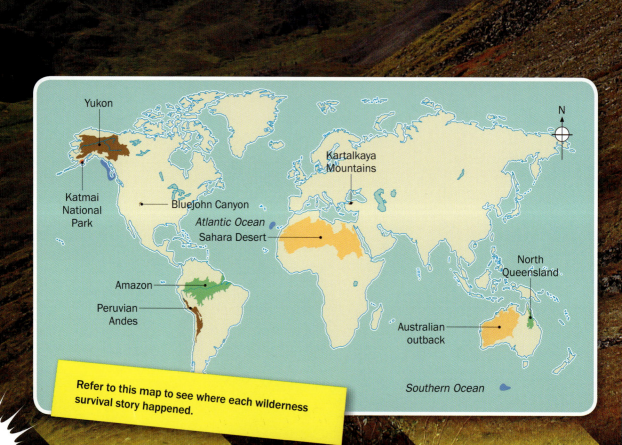

N

Yukon

Kartalkaya
Mountains

Katmai
National
Park

BlueJohn Canyon

Atlantic Ocean

Sahara Desert

North
Queensland

Amazon

Peruvian
Andes

Australian
outback

Southern Ocean

Refer to this map to see where each wilderness
survival story happened.

As the story of Aron Ralston shows, when people explore the wilderness, there are lots of things that can go wrong. They can have accidents, get lost, be pursued by animals, and more. People who have survived in dangerous wilderness areas have had to think clearly about their situations. Like Aron, they must ask themselves: "What can I do to survive?"

Survival skills

This book will look at more stories like Aron's, in which people have fought to survive in the wilderness. Usually wilderness areas are large and **uninhabited** (without people), and are often populated by wild animals. There are lots of different types of wilderness: jungles, forests, mountains, seas, deserts, and even space. Each of these places has different dangers, so, in addition to basic survival skills, people need different sets of skills to survive in each of them.

Be prepared

One of the most important aspects of surviving in the wilderness is preparation. If people are not prepared properly for the environment that they are going into, they may not survive—as we will see with several stories in this book. Just having basic equipment, appropriate clothing, water, and food can mean the difference between life and death. Knowing details about the area is also essential.

Another important aspect of surviving in the wilderness is coping mentally. If people become lost or stranded in an unfamiliar environment, it is very important that they remain calm. It is important to focus at all times on how to survive.

Read the stories in this book to learn how different people have faced different wilderness challenges. How do you think you would cope if your car broke down in the middle of the Australian **outback**, or if you were stranded all alone in the middle of the ocean? Would you stay calm, or would you panic?

The wilderness can be a beautiful and stunning place, but you have to be careful as you explore.

SURVIVING IN THE MOUNTAINS

*In 1985 two British friends, Joe Simpson and Simon Yates, faced a struggle for survival in one of the most dangerous and **remote** (far-off) areas of wilderness on Earth. The two had decided that they wanted to be the first people to climb to the **summit** (highest point) of one of South America's highest mountains, Siula Grande, in Peru. The mountain is nearly 6,400 meters (21,000 feet) high at its peak, and previous attempts to climb it had been abandoned.*

When Joe and Simon set out on their **ascent**, the weather was sunny. They expected that it would take them a couple of days to climb to the top, and then a day to climb back down. They had experience climbing mountains in Europe, but they had never attempted to climb such a tall mountain.

The climb to the top of the mountain was more difficult than the pair had imagined it would be. As they neared the summit, the weather changed suddenly, and they were caught up in a fierce snowstorm. They continued to climb, but

Siula Grande, in the Peruvian Andes, is one of the tallest mountains in South America.

in the cold, windy conditions they did not cover much distance. Their ascent became more and more difficult. As it began to get dark, with the storm still raging, the two climbers decided to stop and dig themselves a **snow hole** to take shelter in overnight.

Reaching the summit

The two climbers made it to the summit of Siula Grande the next day. With much clearer skies, they were able to climb the few hundred feet to the top of the mountain more easily. They spent a small amount of time taking in the views, and then began their **descent** down the mountain. They decided to climb down the mountain in a different direction than the way they had climbed up. They were essentially climbing into the unknown. Expecting that it would take them only one day to reach the bottom, Joe and Simon were shocked to find that descending the mountain was just as tough as climbing up it. They managed to cover only about 300 meters (1,000 feet) on the first day of their descent.

Terrible accident

Disaster struck on the second day of the climbers' descent. As they were slowly climbing down, Joe had a severe accident. His snow axe slipped from the ice, and he was suddenly falling down the mountain. He landed in a heap, with the power of the impact shattering one of his legs. With a long way to go to the bottom of the mountain, Joe did not think he could make it.

Simon made his way down to where Joe was lying. He had to make a decision: leave his friend behind, or try to get them both down the mountain. He quickly decided that he might be able to help Joe down the mountain by lowering him in stages.

Painful descent

As the snow and wind whipped around him, Simon made a solid seat for himself in the snow and lowered his friend down the mountain. When Simon had lowered Joe the full length of the rope, Joe then had to dig himself into the snow and wait for Simon to climb down to meet him. As Joe was being lowered, his broken leg kept catching on the mountainside and causing him almost unbearable pain.

As they neared the point on the mountain where the angle was less steep, Simon lowered Joe

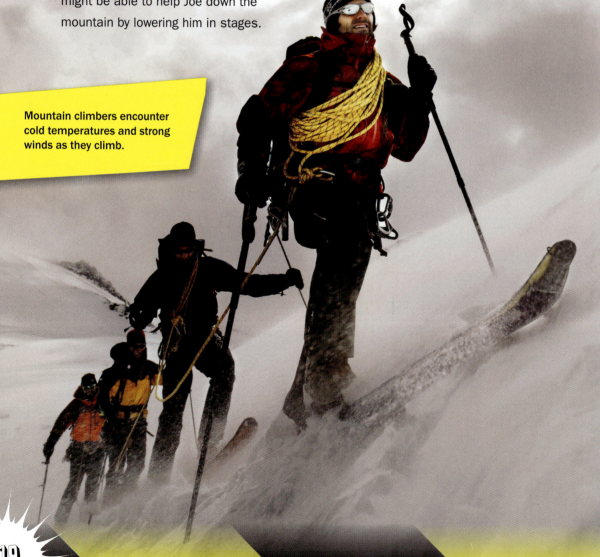

Mountain climbers encounter cold temperatures and strong winds as they climb.

for the last time. Unfortunately, Simon could not see that he was lowering his friend over the side of a ridge. Joe ended up hanging—dangling from the rope—over a deep hole called a **crevasse**.

Cold, injured, and unable to move, Joe just hung there. Weather conditions made it impossible for the two men to talk to each other, so Simon was totally unaware of his friend's position. He was just waiting for the signal that Joe had dug himself safely into the mountain. Eventually the weight of holding Joe became too much, and Simon began to be pulled down the mountain.

Simon knew they would soon both fall off the mountain to their deaths. He had to make the horrifying decision to cut the rope to save his own life.

Waterproof jacket with hood

Goggles

Snow axe

Thermal gloves

SURVIVAL SCIENCE

Altitude sickness

Mountain climbers commonly experience **altitude** sickness (also called acute mountain sickness). It affects people as they move to a higher altitude. The symptoms include:

- mild, flu-like symptoms
- nausea
- hyperventilation (breathing rapidly)
- exhaustion

These symptoms are all the result of a lack of the gas **oxygen** at higher altitudes. The best way to recover is to drop 300 meters (1,000 feet). If not dealt with quickly, altitude sickness can lead to cerebral edema (the brain filling up with fluid) or pulmonary edema (the lungs filling up with fluid). If this happens, the climber will die.

Along with survival skills, climbers need the proper gear to get up and down a mountain safely. Here are some of the basic pieces of equipment.

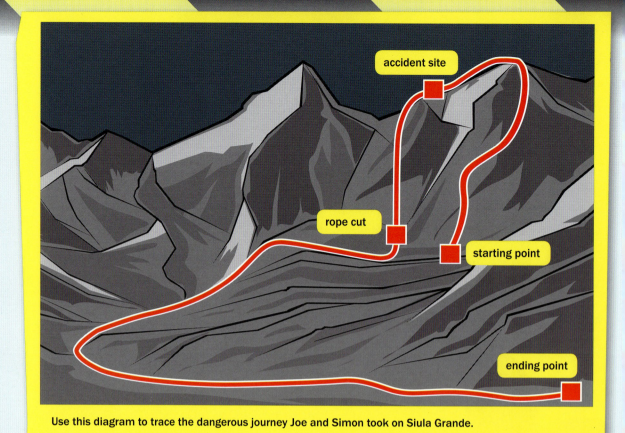

Use this diagram to trace the dangerous journey Joe and Simon took on Siula Grande.

Cutting the rope

Joe had been hanging for more than 90 minutes, waiting for Simon to realize his situation. Suddenly, after Simon cut the rope, Joe was falling again. He fell straight through some ice and down into a ridge in the crevasse. He had survived the fall, but he was now stuck in a hole. He had no food or water and did not think he would make it out. He spent the night shivering and crying, waiting for the cold to kill him.

Simon was devastated. By cutting the rope to save his own life, he thought he had killed his friend. Exhausted, he dug himself a snow hole in which to rest. He had also run out of water, so he needed to get down the mountain as soon as he could the next day.

In the morning, as he made his way down the mountain, Simon arrived at the crevasse. He looked very deep inside it, but could not believe that Joe would have survived the fall. Wracked with guilt, he continued down the mountain and back to base camp.

Determined to survive

Meanwhile, suffering from **hypothermia** (low body temperature; see the box on page 37), **frostbite** (see the box on page 15), and a badly broken leg, Joe was determined to try to survive. He managed to lower himself deeper into the crevasse, looking for a way out. To his relief he reached a point where he could see a hole that led back to the mountainside. He managed to climb out through the hole.

He was still in a desperate position, needing to get to the bottom of the mountain yet unable to use both legs. Because of his lack of water, he was **hallucinating**, or seeing things that were not really there. He fell down often in his trek back to base camp, but he kept going, every step as painful as the last.

As he got closer to base camp, Joe cried out Simon's name, hoping that his friend would hear him and help. Thankfully, Simon did hear him and was overwhelmed with relief that his friend had survived.

With their ordeal nearly over, the two British climbers still had to get out of the mountainous area. They had a painful two-day journey by donkey and then on to Peru's capital, Lima, where Joe could get treatment in a hospital. Amazingly, he made a full recovery.

BEST SELLER

When he returned to Great Britain, Joe Simpson decided to write a book about his ordeal. It became a best seller and was turned into an award-winning movie in 2003, called *Touching the Void*. The movie re-enacts the determination and bravery that both men showed to survive.

This photo is from the movie based on Joe Simpson's book. An actor re-enacts Joe's experience of being lowered down the mountain by rope. This experience was very painful, because his injured leg kept getting caught on the snow and ice as he slid down.

Skiing into trouble

As a member of the U.S. Air Force, Mike Couillard had been given basic survival training. But he did not realize that this training would keep him and his son alive for 10 days in the freezing wilderness.

In January 1995, Mike was stationed on a U.S. air base in Turkey. On one of his days off, he decided to take his 10-year-old son, Matt, on a skiing trip in the nearby mountains. While they were traveling up the mountain on the ski lift, it began to snow. As they began to ski down, the snow started to fall much more heavily, until the two of them could not see more than 1 meter (3.3 feet) ahead. Instead of stopping to take shelter, they kept skiing, hoping to get to the bottom of the mountain before it got dark.

Unfortunately, they were not only caught in the thick snowfall. They were also skiing in the wrong direction. The heavy snow had **disorientated** them, and they were skiing further away from safety. As it began to get dark, they both realized that they would have to spend the night on the mountain. Using the basic survival skills that he had been taught, Mike built a small shelter to keep him and his son **insulated** from the snow and the cold ground.

The Kartalkaya mountain range in Turkey looks beautiful and inviting on a clear day. But a heavy snowstorm can turn this peaceful scene deadly!

Finding shelter

The next day, Mike was lucky to find a different type of shelter. It was a hollow under a tree that was just big enough for the two of them. He said later: "If we had not found that, we would have been [probably] a lot worse off." They had originally set out for a day of skiing, so they had no food or water. There was a stream near the shelter, and it was their only source of water. Mike's training had included advice on drinking water to slow down the onset of frostbite (see the box for more on frostbite). Drinking water can help to keep the body's circulation working, even in the cold.

SURVIVAL SCIENCE

Frostbite

Frostbite can affect the body when it is exposed to very cold temperatures for an extended length of time. Here are some details about frostbite:

- Frostbite mainly affects the extremities of the body, like the nose, fingers, and toes.
- Ice crystals form under the skin, and the body tissue begins to freeze. Feeling is lost around the affected area and it turns black.
- To relieve frostbite, the affected area can be slowly warmed using skin contact or lukewarm water.
- When the frostbite begins to thaw, the pain can be unbearable. People who have suffered from frostbite have compared the thawing of the skin to 10 times the pain of severe sunburn.

Severe frostbite requires urgent medical assistance.

False hope

Mike knew that people would realize that he and his son were missing. On the second day, when he heard helicopters overhead, he thought that they would be rescued. He tried to use his credit card to reflect the sun and draw the attention of the helicopter crews, but this did not work. Mike later admitted that when he heard the helicopters, he got excited, thinking that he and his son would be rescued. But he then became very depressed when he realized that they had not been spotted.

Tough decision

After spending eight cold nights on the mountain in their fight for survival, Mike honestly thought that he and Matt would die there. He even wrote a short note to his wife, telling her how much he loved her. He had to make a decision: to stay where they were and die, or to leave Matt behind and try to get some help. He decided to try to find help.

After making the agonizing decision to leave his 10-year-old son behind, Mike struggled for a couple of miles until he found some empty huts. It was starting to get dark, and he was totally exhausted, with no energy to go back for his son. He settled down in the hut for the night. He could not sleep because his frostbite was causing him a lot of pain, and because he could not stop thinking about Matt all alone on the mountain.

A search party of Turkish commandos and U.S. military volunteers prepares to go into the mountains to search for Mike and Matt.

While they recovered in the hospital, Mike Couillard and his son Matt were reunited with the rest of their family.

Struggling on

The next day Mike wanted to go back to his son, but he could not move because he was so tired and in so much pain. On the second day in the hut, Mike thought that he heard movement and voices nearby. He used all the strength he had left to leave the hut and managed to get the attention of some local lumberjacks passing by. He was in a terrible state and unable to communicate properly. Eventually he managed to tell the men that his son was still on the mountain, and so they set off to find him.

One hour later, Mike was reunited with his son, and the two of them were helped down the mountain. This grueling physical and emotional experience left them both in need of medical attention. They had to spend more than two months in the hospital. Matt lost one of his toes to frostbite, and both received counseling to help deal with the stress of the event. Together they managed to get through their ordeal and recover fully.

SURVIVING IN THE FOREST

Katmai National Park, on the southern coast of Alaska, is a beautiful area of rugged wilderness. The stunning surroundings include mountains, lakes, and forests that are home to brown bears, also known as grizzly bears. These large, wild bears live in the national park, hibernating in the winter months and hunting in the summer.

Living with the bears

In the summer of 1989, Timothy Treadwell, a man from California, visited the park and immediately fell in love with the bears that he saw there. The following summer, despite having no experience or survival training, he made the decision to go and live in the wilderness, among the bears.

For 13 summers, Timothy spent his time camping in Katmai National Park. He wanted to study the bears and raise awareness about the destruction of their natural **habitat** and the danger caused by people hunting bears illegally. He took photos and videos of the bears as they hunted, played, fought, and mated during the summer months.

Timothy Treadwell, with his camera equipment for filming the bears in their natural environment.

The more time that Timothy spent with the bears in their wild environment, the closer he became to them. He forged a strange kind of bond with some of the bears, giving them names and often getting so close to them that he could reach out and touch them. Grizzly bears have been known to **decapitate** (cut the head off of) a human with one swipe of a powerful paw! Timothy was aware of these dangers, and he was often quoted as saying that he could die in this environment if he was not careful.

Katmai National Park, in Alaska, is home to lots of different wildlife including grizzly bears.

Risky behavior?

The local people and the authorities who ran the national park were divided in their opinion of Timothy and his unusual lifestyle. Some of them were concerned that living among the bears could unsettle the bears in their natural habitat. The superintendent of the national park, Deb Liggett, was quoted as saying of Timothy, "At best he is misguided. At worst he is dangerous."

Raising awareness

But others were pleased that Timothy was drawing attention to the problems faced by the bears. When he was not studying the bears, he would often spend time in schools talking to students about the bears.

Timothy Treadwell is seen here getting very close to the bears so that he can capture them on film.

Because of his unusual lifestyle, Timothy became a celebrity and appeared on television talk shows. He used these appearances to try to make people understand why he was living in the wilderness with the grizzly bears. He also set up a foundation called "Grizzly People" to help raise awareness.

Tragic end

The thirteenth summer that Timothy spent with the bears was his last. A pilot spotted the bodies of Timothy and his girlfriend, Anne Huguenard, as he flew over the area near their camp. The two had been violently attacked and killed by a large brown bear. It is thought that the bear had struggled to find enough food to survive and had killed and eaten Timothy and Anne because he was starving.

No one knows exactly what happened. It must have been a shocking and horrifying final few moments for Timothy and Anne. But these tragic deaths could easily have been prevented. It certainly serves as a reminder about the unpredictability of wild animals, and the potential danger in trying to protect them in their natural habitat.

SURVIVAL TIPS

Surviving a bear attack

If you ever find yourself in the wilderness, confronted by a bear, there are a few simple rules to remember to avoid being attacked and killed:

- ✔ Try to stay downwind of bears, so that they cannot smell you. Bears use scent to hunt.
- ✔ Don't be tempted to get too close to a bear in the wild.
- ✔ Never approach a mother with her cubs. She will become very aggressive.
- ✔ Never run. Bears can run faster than humans and are excited by the chase.
- ✔ Do not climb a tree. Bears can climb better than humans.
- ✔ If you cannot get away from the bear, then you might still survive by pretending to be dead. Lie on the ground and try not to move. You might be able to fool the bear.

Yukon adventure

Ed Wardle, a British television cameraman, director, and producer, had traveled to many different areas of the world during his career, including South America and Africa. He had also worked in extreme conditions like the North Pole and Mount Everest. Nothing, though, could have prepared him for his astonishing trip into the wilderness of the Yukon, in northern Canada, in 2009.

The Yukon is a stunning and isolated area of wilderness. It includes forests, rivers, and mountains.

Big plans!

Ed planned to demonstrate what might happen to an average person if that person had to survive alone in a harsh environment. He prepared for the expedition for over a year, but to keep the demonstration as realistic as possible, he intentionally avoided learning specific survival methods for the Yukon environment. He planned to be dropped into the area with only basic equipment, including an axe, shotgun, hammock, and canoe. He also had lots of camera equipment, since he would film his adventure for a television company. The goal was for him to stay in the area for three months and try to survive.

As soon as Ed arrived, he said, "I knew it was going to be a big, tough, long haul both physically and mentally. But as soon as I landed on the lake and the plane took off, I was overwhelmed by it. I thought: 'What have I got myself into?'" The area of Yukon wilderness that he was in was 160 kilometers (100 miles) away from the nearest town. He was in a forested area surrounded by mountains, with streams, rivers, and lakes nearby.

Not according to plan

As in any survival situation, finding food was an immediate concern. Ed knew that the laws of Canada prevented him from hunting large animals like moose and caribou, as well as many other fur-bearing animals. Because of this, he had planned to fish for much of his food. At that time of year, the rivers would usually have been full of salmon, but because of unusually high temperatures, their arrival in the area had been delayed. Eventually Ed was forced to survive by eating porcupines.

NEAREST TOWN 100 MILES!

Ed Wardle had to catch and eat porcupines. They are difficult to catch, and not very nice to eat.

Starvation

Toward the end of his trip, Ed was eating only once every two days. The muscles in his body began to waste away, and his heart rate dropped because he was starving. He would not have lasted very much longer without food (see box below).

SURVIVAL SCIENCE

Starvation

All humans need food to survive. The food that we eat is full of vitamins and nutrients that help the body's **vital organs**, such as the heart, kidneys, and liver, function properly. But in a survival situation, the body needs calories (energy) from food most of all. Without enough calories the body will use up fat reserves and then muscles will start to waste away. Vital muscles like the heart will eventually begin to fail, too. This extreme lack of food is often called starvation. The longer that a person goes without food, the worse effect starvation will have on the body.

The physical symptoms of starvation include:
- dizziness
- weakness
- low body temperature
- low blood pressure

The emotional effects of starvation include:
- depression
- anger
- irritability
- anxiety

If the human body does not get the calories, vitamins, and nutrients it needs, it will eventually begin to shut down, leading to death.

Scared and alone

Along with the physical problems that he was suffering, Ed began to fall apart mentally. He was keeping a video diary of his trip for the television program, and as the days passed his attitude in the videos started to change. From being at first positive and excited about his adventure in the wilderness, he was becoming depressed about his situation. He was scared, lonely, and miserable and was having difficulty motivating himself. In the last of the videos, he broke down in tears. After 50 days, Ed had to contact his support team, who immediately came and rescued him.

First rule of survival

Even though Ed did not complete the full 90 day expedition, the fact that he was able to survive for 50 days is still impressive. Though he had avoided becoming an expert in Yukon survival, Ed had prepared an emergency exit strategy and communications system. Because of this, it was possible to rescue him when his situation became desperate.

Ed's story is unique, because he wanted to show what could happen without full survival preparation. To survive in the wilderness, it is essential to know about the area and all of the different things that can be eaten to survive.

After recovering back in Britain, Ed said that he would return to the Yukon, but under different circumstances. He said: "I would go back—but for two weeks and take a lot of food and a lot of friends with me."

Ed Wardle in the Yukon wilderness, during the 50 days he survived there.

SURVIVING IN THE OUTBACK

The **outback** is the name given to the inland area of Australia. This huge area of wilderness covers about 6.5 million square kilometers (2.5 million square miles). The average temperature in the outback in the summer is a hot 35°C (95°F), but some days the temperature can reach up to 45°C (113°F). The land is made up of mountainous areas and large deserts.

Traveling into the outback

In December 1998, in the middle of the Australian summer, two Austrian tourists picked up a 4x4 rental car and traveled down from Sydney to South Australia. Karl Goeschka and his girlfriend, Caroline Grossmueller, had decided to visit Lake Eyre in the outback. They set out from their base in South Australia to William Creek.

From William Creek, the couple then traveled the 61 kilometers (40 miles) to Lake Eyre. They slept in their vehicle, and in the morning they realized that during the night a strong wind had blown sand all around it, so they could not drive away. To try to get them moving, Karl let some air out of the car's tires.

SURVIVAL TIPS

Tire footprints

When driving in a sandy desert, it is a good idea to let some air out of your tires—to about half of their regular pressure. As you let air out of the tire, the area (or footprint) of the tire expands and has more **traction** (grip) against the sand. This creates more friction between the tire and the road surface. The more friction there is, the better the chance of being able to drive on sand or other loose surfaces.

Stranded

Unfortunately, Karl did not let enough air out of the tires (see box at left). The vehicle was still stranded. He then tried to remove the sand from around the vehicle, but this was difficult without a shovel. Still, they had lots of food and 65 liters (17 gallons) of water. Very nearby there was a water tank that held about 300 liters (80 gallons) of water. They certainly had enough food and water to survive for weeks—if they stayed where they were.

The Australian outback is very dry and it is one of the hottest places on Earth.

Tragic mistakes

After three days in temperatures that exceeded 40°C (104°F), and without seeing another vehicle, Karl and Caroline decided to try to walk the 61 kilometers (40 miles) back to William Creek. They were concerned that no one was aware that they were missing, so no one would come to look for them. They set off with as much water as they could carry and began to walk late in the afternoon, when the temperature was not as high.

SURVIVAL TIPS

Keep in touch

The police recommend that if you are traveling in the wilderness, you choose a friend or family member who will know exactly where you are going. That person can contact the authorities if you are not back by a certain time.

This man's vehicle has broken down in the outback. He is using his cell phone to try to get some help.

The couple walked for five hours, using up one-third of their water, before they stopped to rest. They rested for five hours and then started walking again. They lasted only one hour before Karl collapsed with exhaustion. At this point the best decision they could have made would have been to return to their vehicle and wait.

But they decided to split up. Caroline was sure that she could walk the remaining distance back to William Creek. She took 9 liters (2.4 gallons) of water and set off. Karl took time to regain his strength, and then made his way back to the car. Tragically, they never saw each other again.

Too late

Six days later, a German couple traveling along the route found Caroline's body by the side of the road. Experts believe she lasted for only one day after splitting up with Karl. She had traveled only half of the distance to William Creek. Caroline had not taken enough water with her to survive, and when the water ran out she became very tired and **disorientated**. Without any water, her **vital organs** shut down, and she died (see box below).

EXHIBIT GG4.

HELP!

Had to leave boyfriend alone due to health problems with less water. (~5-10 km past sign (WC 50) - direction Lake Eyre.

Myself still trying to get out of this hell heading towards William Creek, which 2 inhabitans simply forgot us.

Please try to find us!

This letter, desperately asking for help, was found near Caroline's body.

SURVIVAL SCIENCE

Dehydration

When the body loses too much water and begins to shut down, the condition is called **dehydration**. If a person cannot, or does not, drink enough water, the effects of severe dehydration can be serious and sometimes lead to death. The symptoms of severe dehydration are:

- severe thirst
- dry skin
- inability to urinate
- irritability
- sunken eyes

- a weak pulse
- a rapid heartbeat
- cold hands and feet
- body seizures
- loss of consciousness

Police found Karl alive, back at the car. Knowing exactly how much air to remove from the tires, it took a police officer only 10 minutes to get the vehicle out of the sand. This was a sad reminder of the importance of being trained before entering the wilderness.

SURVIVING IN THE DESERT

Mauro Prosperi is an Italian policeman. He is also a runner. He competed at the 1984 Olympics, winning a gold medal in the **pentathlon**. In 1994 he took part in the Marathon des Sables ("Marathon of the Sands") in the Sahara Desert for the first time. The Marathon des Sables is a yearly event held in Morocco, North Africa. It is a test of physical **endurance** that covers five marathons in six days, in temperatures up to 49˚C (120˚F). The event covers a total distance of 243 kilometers (151 miles).

The Marathon des Sables is a very popular event. It is a real test of physical and mental endurance, in some of the hottest temperatures on Earth.

On the third day of the race, after leaving a checkpoint in seventh place, Mauro was caught up in a sandstorm. The sandstorm struck suddenly and made it impossible to see the route of the race. Mauro tried to continue running, but he found it impossible and eventually stopped. He found some shelter under a bush. When the sandstorm stopped, he realized that he was no longer on the route of the race and was lost. At the end of the day, all of the other competitors made it to the final checkpoint. Only Mauro was missing.

Lost!

The next day the organizers of the marathon sent people out to search for him. A helicopter was also sent out to search, but could not find him. Mauro had very little water or other supplies with him. When his water ran out, he decided that instead of dying a slow, painful death in the desert, he would use his penknife to slit his wrists and kill himself. He later said, "All I could think about was that I was going to die a horrible death. I had once heard that dying of thirst was the worst possible fate."

So, he slit his wrists and soon fell asleep. But because of **dehydration**, his blood coagulated (clotted) around the cuts he had made. This saved his life, and he awoke the next day with a new determination to survive.

Staying alive

Mauro had become **disorientated** during the sandstorm. When he started to run again, it was in the wrong direction, away from the area where the marathon was being held. He ran for days, covering more than 160 kilometers (100 miles). He had to drink his own urine to avoid total dehydration, and he attempted to stay out of the sun during the hottest part of the day. The temperature in the desert drops significantly at night, and so Mauro buried himself in the sand to keep warm. In order to survive, he managed to catch and kill bats, lizards, and snakes—eating them and drinking their blood.

Saved!

On the ninth day of his ordeal, Mauro was found by a group of Tuareg nomads (see box at right) who lived in the desert. They took him by camel to the nearest village, where he was able to recover. He had actually trekked for about 210 kilometers (130 miles) in the wrong direction and ended up in a different country, Algeria (see the map). During his time in the desert, Mauro had lost more than 13 kilograms (30 pounds) of body weight, and his liver was severely damaged. But, incredibly, he had survived. He came back from the point of suicide to show an immense amount of courage and determination to survive.

Years later, after recovering fully, Mauro returned to the Sahara and completed the Marathon des Sables. He has now completed the race six times. On his return to the desert he said, "I am a competitor, and I love the desert."

This map shows the planned route of the race, and where Mauro began running in the wrong direction.

LIVING IN THE WILDERNESS: THE TUAREG

The Tuareg are a nomadic tribe that lives in the Sahara Desert, in North Africa. Nomads have no permanent home, but rather travel with the change of seasons in search of new land to farm. There are approximately 900,000 Tuareg. The Tuareg farm their own crops, including barley, wheat, corn, onions, tomatoes, and dates. They also keep camels, goats, cattle, and chickens that graze the land.

Tuareg men often cover their faces with an indigo-blue-dyed cloth, and so they are often referred to as the "Blue Men" or "Blue Men of the Desert."

SURVIVING AT SEA

The surface of Earth is made up of 71 percent water. If you get lost at sea, then you are lost in the largest wilderness on the planet.

Yacht race disaster

In 1997, while taking part in the Vendée Globe, an around-the-world yacht race, Englishman Tony Bullimore found himself fighting for his life, hundreds of miles from anywhere. Tony was a very experienced sailor and ex-marine who had sailed across the Atlantic Ocean more than 40 times. In 1985 he was named "Yachtsman of the Year."

The Vendée Globe is one of the toughest yachting races in the world. Only a small number of brave competitors have ever completed this solo race across the world's oceans. During the 1997 race, in the Southern Ocean between Antarctica and Australia, Tony's yacht was caught in a major storm.

The storm raged for hours, with winds of up to 160 kilometers per hour (100 miles per hour) and massive waves that crashed into the yacht. The storm seemed to be getting worse and worse, until there was a loud crack and the yacht **capsized** (overturned) almost instantly. Tony later said: "In those conditions, if you don't know what you're doing, you'd be dead in five or ten minutes."

Stranded

The capsized yacht was in the middle of the ice-cold Southern Ocean, 2,500 kilometers (1,550 miles) off the coast of Australia. Tony set off his radio distress beacon and desperately waited to be rescued. Although the yacht had capsized, Tony was able to survive in a small air pocket inside the overturned hull (main body of the boat).

It was bitterly cold, though, and he was soon suffering from **hypothermia** and **frostbite**. He also had very little drinking water, and when that ran out he suffered from **dehydration**. He just hoped that someone had picked up his distress signal and that help was on the way.

"In those conditions, if you don't know what you're doing, you'd be dead in five or ten minutes." —Tony Bullimore

Rough, dangerous storms are one of the many challenges that yacht racers must face during the Vendée Globe.

Cold and alone

Tony spent five days freezing in the small air pocket. He was lonely and cold. After so many sailing adventures, he was now facing the biggest challenge of his life: staying alive. He later said: "You're only interested in survival. After three or four days I'd come to the conclusion that I wasn't going to be rescued, but you can't just give up." On the fifth day, with **oxygen** running out in his air pocket, he heard knocking on the outside of the yacht and then heard voices. He was exhausted, but used his remaining energy to swim out from under the yacht.

Tony Bullimore's yacht had capsized and was drifting in the freezing ocean.

An exhausted Tony Bullimore, immediately after being rescued.

Members of the Australian Navy greeted Tony as he emerged from the yacht. They had been alerted to his position by the distress beacon. The crew of the naval rescue helicopter took him back to the HMAS *Adelaide*. Once on board, he was taken care of and given a cup of tea. The ship took him to Perth, in southwest Australia, where he was able to fully recover.

SURVIVAL SCIENCE

Hypothermia

When a person's body temperature falls below 35°C (95°F) the condition is called hypothermia. Different situations will determine how badly people are affected by hypothermia. In the worst cases of hypothermia, the symptoms include:

- loss of control of hands, feet, and limbs
- body stops shivering (meaning heat is no longer being generated)
- stiff muscles
- dilated pupils (meaning that the pupil, the small black circle in the center of the eye, gets larger)
- unconsciousness

If a person is suffering from any form of hypothermia, it is very important that he or she tries to stay as warm and **insulated** as possible. If the person continues to get colder, the body will eventually shut down, and the person will die.

Saved but not unscathed!

Tony had survived in the freezing cold Southern Ocean, but he did not escape unscathed. One of his fingers had been cut off during his ordeal, and he also lost two toes to frostbite. He also had to recover from hypothermia. It took months for him to fully regain the feeling in his hands and feet.

While Tony was stranded, experts had thought that his chances of survival were only about 10 percent. He was extremely lucky to survive this terrifying experience, and amazingly it did not prevent him from wanting to sail again. As soon as he felt well enough, he was back on a boat and racing again. He has since sailed around the world three times.

Lost at sea

In 1982 American Steve Callahan had sailed alone from the United States to Britain, in a boat that he built himself, to take part in a sailing competition. He started the race, but was delayed because his boat needed to be repaired. He spent time repairing his boat on the Canary Islands, off the coast of northwest Africa, before he set off back across the Atlantic Ocean to the United States. Steve designed ships and was a moderately experienced sailor.

Steve Callahan on his boat, before setting sail back to the United States.

Crash!

Steve had been sailing for about a week and had covered about 1,300 kilometers (800 miles), when he suddenly heard a loud noise that sounded like an explosion. There was a large hole in the boat, possibly caused by a whale crashing into it. Seawater started to rush into the boat, and Steve had to make the immediate decision to leave the boat. He quickly grabbed his survival kit. He launched his emergency raft and watched as his boat capsized and sank. He was now alone in his emergency raft, in the Atlantic Ocean.

SURVIVAL SCIENCE

Drinking seawater

When a person drinks seawater, the amount of salt in the body increases. As a result, water is taken from the blood into the urine by the kidneys to help the body get rid of the extra salt. Water then moves out of the cells of the body to keep the concentration of the blood stable. So the cells become dehydrated and the body doesn't work properly. People become dehydrated more quickly by drinking seawater than by not drinking anything at all!

Considering his situation, Steve was quite well prepared. In his survival kit he had 8 pints (3.8 liters) of water, 2 **solar stills** (which can be used to convert seawater into drinking water; see the box), a knife, flares, some food, and a spear gun. The solar stills and the spear gun would be crucial for his survival.

Steve was aware that his chances were slim, though, and initially thought to himself: "Forget it. You are not going to get out of here." But he knew that most people who had survived at sea for a long time had prepared properly. He hoped that with his raft and survival kit he had a chance. Using his sailing experience, he figured out that he could cross the Atlantic in his raft in two and a half to three months. He anticipated that the natural ocean currents and winds would take him from his starting point across to the Caribbean.

Staying disciplined

Steve knew that it was important to stay disciplined. He **rationed** the water that he had, drinking only a mouthful every few hours to prevent dehydration. He set up his solar stills to collect more drinking water. He struggled with them at first. Every time that he would collect some salt-free water, a wave would crash into the still, knocking it over and carrying away his precious drinking water. Eventually, he managed to overcome this.

In addition to water, he knew that when the food in his survival kit ran out, he would have to use the spear gun to catch some fish to eat. Although Steve was surrounded by an ocean full of fish, he struggled for two weeks before he managed to spear one. When he did catch one, he was overjoyed.

Steve was in a very difficult situation, but he kept telling himself that he was doing the best he could. He figured out a routine for his days, which included exercising in the mornings to try to stay fit and healthy. On his 43rd day on the raft, he speared a fish, but the spear broke and the fish swam directly at the raft, ripping a hole in it. The raft began to take on water, but Steve managed to keep a clear head. After a couple of attempts, he was able to use a piece of cork to fill the hole in the raft and bound it in place. He also managed to fix the spear so that he could still catch fish to eat.

How far?

Steve knew that he had traveled quite a long way in his raft, but he was concerned that he might not make it to the Caribbean. He needed to figure out as accurately as possible how far he had traveled. Using his knowledge and experience, he managed to estimate that he had covered about 2,250 kilometers (1,400 miles). All that he could do now was hope that the current and the wind would continue to take him west toward the islands of the Caribbean and not north, further into the ocean.

On the 75th night of his ordeal, Steve noticed the light from a lighthouse in the distance. The following day, local fisherman rescued him. He had survived for two and a half months alone at sea. He had managed to stay calm during some very scary moments, and he had used his knowledge and experience to survive in the biggest wilderness on Earth.

After being rescued, Steve demonstrated how he used his spear gun to catch fish. If he had not been able to fish successfully, he probably would have starved.

SURVIVING IN THE JUNGLE

In 1971, a 17-year-old German girl named Juliane Margaret Koepcke was the only survivor of a plane crash in the Amazon, in South America. The plane was flying over the jungle when it was struck by lightning and broke up in the air. Juliane had fallen over 3 kilometers (about 2 miles) into the jungle, but her only serious injury was a broken collarbone. Although she had survived the plane crash, she still had to try to survive in the jungle.

Using her knowledge

Juliane was lucky because she had some knowledge about the jungle. She had spent time in the jungle with her parents, who ran a wildlife research center in the Peruvian Amazon. One of the most important lessons that her father had taught her was that if you find a creek, follow it because that will lead to a stream, and a stream will lead to a bigger river—and the river will lead to people. On her second day in the jungle, she found a stream and followed her father's advice.

One of the most important lessons to learn for survival in the jungle is to build a shelter above the ground. This keeps a person from being bitten or stung by the many insects that live on the jungle floor. Juliane did this, but unfortunately cuts on her arms had already become infested with **parasites**, living things which live and feed on other living things and damage their host.

Found

On her ninth day in the jungle, Juliane found a small, empty hut on the bank of a river, where she spent the night. The following day lumberjacks arrived at the hut. She then faced a long canoe journey up the river before she was taken to a hospital, where she made a full recovery.

When the authorities arrived at the plane's crash site, they discovered that Juliane had not been the only survivor of the crash. They believed that as many as 14 people had survived initially, but they died because they did not know how to survive in the jungle.

The Amazon jungle is a vast and dangerous area to be lost in.

WORKING IN THE WILDERNESS

*Trying to survive in the wilderness is usually something that happens while exploring a **remote** area. But sometimes people get pulled into survival situations as part of their work.*

In August 2007, while working on his huge cattle farm in North Queensland, Australia, David George was thrown from his horse. He was knocked unconscious. When he woke up a few hours later, his head was bleeding. He was confused and **disorientated**, but he thought that if he could just get back on his horse, it would take him home.

The horse took a different route, though, into a swamp area infested with crocodiles. Before he had the chance to turn back, David stumbled upon a large crocodile nest. Believing he was in danger from the many crocodiles in the area, he decided to try to find some higher ground. David managed to climb up a tree, and he sat there for the whole night. He was uncomfortable and aware of being stalked by a couple of large crocodiles.

Signaling for help

After surviving the first night up the tree, David decided that he would stay where he was rather than risk going near the crocodiles. He knew that someone would have alerted the authorities to the fact that he was missing, so he would just wait to be rescued.

Australian farmer David George thanks his rescuers from the Australian Army.

As the days passed, David could see planes and helicopters searching overhead. He tried his best to attract their attention. He used his shirt as a flag and tried to reflect the sunlight off a small metal can he had with him. Eventually one of the pilots of an Australian Army helicopter noticed the sunlight being reflected and spotted him. David was pulled to safety from the tree.

Six nights in the tree

David had survived in the tree for six nights. He had had two meat sandwiches on him when he fell from his horse, and he had been lucky that there was moisture on the tree that he could drink. He was also lucky to survive being in the crocodiles' natural **habitat** and live to tell his story.

A crocodile could eat a human in seconds!

LIVING IN THE WILDERNESS

The beautiful and rugged coastal area around Alaska and British Columbia.

For a small number of people, the wilderness is where they live. Every day things can go wrong and difficult situations can arise. Experience, knowledge, skill, and mental strength help people to survive living in the wilderness.

Remote coastal wilderness

There are many small communities dotted along the coast of British Columbia and the northern Canada–Alaska border. These communities are in **remote** areas. Depending on the time of year or the weather conditions, these communities can be cut off for weeks or even months at a time. The people who live there have to be totally self-reliant.

The Wortman family lived in one of these remote areas in the 1970s. In order to get food and supplies, they would often travel by boat down the Alaskan coast to Prince Rupert, on the coast of British Columbia, about 190 kilometers (120 miles) away. This was a familiar routine for the family. On one occasion, however, their journey back home became a story of survival.

Shipwrecked

The father (Elmo), his son (Randy), and his two daughters (Cindy and Geana) were traveling back to their home when a storm developed. Strong winds pushed their boat toward the land, and it would have been crushed against the shore. The Wortmans had to abandon their boat, and they ended up stranded on the beach of an **uninhabited** island. It was the middle of winter, and they knew that no one would be looking for them. The family decided to stay positive and try to survive.

The Wortmans built a shelter and started a fire, on which they cooked some mussels that they managed to find. They then settled down for the night. Elmo knew that there was a cabin on an island about 32 kilometers (20 miles) away, and that if they could get there, they might be rescued.

For the Wortman family, life in the coastal wilderness was normal despite the dangers. This photo is a from a movie made about them.

Making a plan

The family had managed to get the lifeboat from the shipwrecked boat, but it was too damaged to carry all four of them. Randy and Geana sailed the lifeboat to another beach nearby, where they hoped to fix it. Meanwhile, Elmo and Cindy had to trek for two days to meet up with them. After fixing the lifeboat well enough to carry the whole family, they set out to reach the cabin. After struggling for over a week, they were still about 10 kilometers (6 miles) from the cabin.

The family decided to split up, so that Elmo and Randy could hopefully get to the cabin quickly and then return to rescue the girls. Initially the family thought they would be reunited in only a few hours, but things did not go according to plan. Elmo and Randy were unable to travel much farther in the lifeboat, because the water had frozen to thick ice. They abandoned the lifeboat and set off on foot, eventually reaching the cabin. Once there they used a **CB radio** to call for help.

Mental strength

Cindy and Geana were all alone, exposed to the cold, and without food for about 13 days before they were rescued. They had to stay positive and continue hoping that their father and brother would survive and come back for them. Geana was only 13 years old at the time, and she showed an immense amount of courage. She and her older sister had to rely on their mental strength and the survival skills that they had learned living in the wilderness.

Elmo, who had spent days recovering from exhaustion and **frostbite** in the cabin, managed to find a small boat and set off to rescue the girls. He hoped that they had survived in the harsh conditions. As he approached the beach where the girls had been left, he was terrified about what he would find. But, amazingly, both of the girls had survived. They all returned to the cabin and were eventually rescued by the coast guard. In all, the girls had spent almost a month without any real food. Their faith, positive attitude, and mental toughness had helped them to stay alive long enough to be rescued.

SURVIVAL TIPS AND ADVICE

As this book has shown, preparation and knowledge are essential when you are visiting a wilderness area. You should always know basic skills, such as how to build a shelter or start a fire. To help you survive if you encounter problems in the wilderness, you should try to avoid getting into a panic. One trick for remaining calm is to remember the letters of the word *stop*:

S: STOP, DON'T PANIC

T: THINK ABOUT YOUR SITUATION

O: ORIENTATE YOURSELF (FIGURE OUT WHERE YOU ARE), OBSERVE YOUR SURROUNDINGS

P: PLAN

Building a shelter

When out in the wilderness, having somewhere to stay that is protected from the wind and rain is very important. When you build your shelter, make sure that it is on solid ground and in a dry, flat area. If you do not have the ability or materials to build a shelter, then you must try to find a natural shelter. Caves or trees with low-hanging branches can make good short-term shelters. If you know that people will be looking for you, try to make your shelter as visible as possible, so that you can be spotted and rescued.

Starting a fire

A fire is a very good source of heat to keep you warm and dry. It can be used to cook food and boil water. A fire can also be used to create smoke signals (see below). If you do not have matches or a lighter with you, you can strike a flint stone with another stone to create a spark, and then a fire. Materials such as dry leaves, dry grass, paper, or even fibers from clothing can be used to start the fire from the spark. Once the fire has started, you can add larger pieces of material and wood to keep the fire going.

Water

Water is the most important ingredient in survival. The human body needs water to survive much more than it needs food. A human can survive for weeks without food, but only about six days without water.

Food

In the wilderness, it is important to take in enough calories to allow your body to work properly and control your body temperature so you can survive until you are rescued. The food that you can eat is dependent on your environment. In most environments, there are plants, insects, and other kinds of animals that you can eat to survive.

Signaling for help

If you are lost in the wilderness, you want to make sure that people have an excellent chance of finding you. Signal fires are a very good idea during the day. If you can find a material that creates a lot of smoke when it burns, then it will create a big cloud of smoke. If you cannot create a fire, try using a mirror or any other reflective material to signal for help. A plane or helicopter searching overhead might see this.

GLOSSARY

altitude height above sea level

amputate cut off all or part of a limb of the body, usually by surgery

ascent act of moving up something, such as a mountain

capsize when a boat overturns in the water

CB Radio (Citizens' Band Radio) two-way radio service for short-distance personal or business communications between fixed or mobile stations

crevasse deep hole in a glacier or other body of ice

decapitate cut the head off of something

dehydration when the body suffers from lack of water

descent act of moving down something, such as a mountain

disorientated having lost your sense of direction because you are confused

endurance ability to suffer an unpleasant or difficult process or situation without giving up

frostbite injury or destruction of skin and underlying tissue that results from continued exposure to freezing temperatures. It most often affects the nose, ears, fingers, or toes.

habitat natural environment for a plant or animal

hallucinating having false or distorted perception of objects or events; imagining things that are not really there

hypothermia unusually low body temperature, often caused by continued exposure to cold

insulate protect from heat, cold, or noise

outback inland wilderness of Australia

oxygen gas that occurs in Earth's atmosphere and water. Many living things need oxygen to breathe.

parasite organism that lives in or on another organism (its host), and benefits by taking nutrients at the other's expense

pentathlon athletic contest with five different track and field events. The competitor with the highest total score after the five events is the winner.

ration to limit the supply of something, particularly food or water. If you know that something needs to last for many days, the supply can be rationed to make it last longer.

remote far-off

snow hole hole dug into the snow, where a person can take shelter from the cold

solar still device that can be used to collect and process drinking water

summit highest point of a mountain

traction grip of a tire on the road surface

uninhabited without people

vital organ organ in the body that is essential for life, such as the heart, kidneys, and liver

FIND OUT MORE

BOOKS

Borgenicht, David, Justin Heimberg, and Chuck Gonzalez. *The Worst-Case Scenario Survival Handbook: Extreme Junior Edition*. San Francisco, CA: Chronicle, 2008.

Boy Scouts of America. Wilderness Survival. Irving, TX: Boy Scouts of America, 2001.

Callahan, Steve. *Adrift: 76 Days Lost at Sea*. Boston, MA: Houghton Mifflin, 2002.

Dowswell, Paul. *True Survival Stories* (*Usborne True Stories* series). Tulsa, OK: EDC, 2008.

George, Jean Craighead et al. *Pocket Guide to the Outdoors*. New York, NY: Dutton, 2009.

Lewis, Simon. *Survival at Sea* (*Difficult and Dangerous* series). Mankato, MN: Smart Apple Media, 2009.

O'Shei, Tim. *How to Survive in the Wilderness* (*Prepare to Survive* series). Mankato, MN: Capstone, 2009.

Piper, Ross. *Survival!: Staying Alive in the Wild* (*Extreme!* series). Mankato, MN: Capstone, 2008.

Ralston, Aron. *Between a Rock and a Hard Place*. New York, NY: Atria Books, 2004.

Simpson, Joe. *Touching the Void*. New York, NY: Perennial, 2004.

DVDS

Grizzly Man. Santa Monica, CA: Lions Gate, 2005.

German filmmaker Werner Herzog used the hundred hours of footage that Timothy Treadwell had filmed to make this movie. It contains some stunning and incredible scenes of Timothy interacting with the bears and other animals.

Wings of Hope. Munich, Germany: Werner Herzog Films, 2000.

Juliane Koepcke's amazing story of survival in the wilderness is included in this film. Herzog follows her as she returns to the jungle.

Touching the Void. Santa Monica, CA: MGM, 2004.

Learn more about the amazing story of Joe Simpson and Simon Yates in this movie.

WEBSITES

www.wilderness-survival-skills.com/survival-preparedness.html

Learn more about basic survival skills at this website.

www.survivaliq.com/survival/introduction.htm

Find out how to survive in a variety of places and situations at this website.

http://channel.nationalgeographic.com/channel/alone-in-the-wild-eds-bio

See videos by Ed Wardle at this National Geographic website.

INDEX